F

MW01206215

Imagine your classroom buzzing with kids fully engaged and invested in their learning. You can make that happen by incorporating simple engagement games, activities and strategies that are sure to make a difference. Go from boring to buzzing!

Providing hands on experiences, engaging games, fun activities and a chance for collaboration will be sure to get your students excited to learn. They will look forward to coming to school as you set the stage for what learning should be like in a classroom. Let your kids experience it now...don't wait!

Don't miss the BONUS in the back of the book. There is a QR Code for a free set of "Levels of Engagement Posters" for the classroom. They help kids understand where they are with classroom engagement and can learn through scenario cards.

TABLE OF CONTENTS

TABLE OF CONTENTS

WHAT IS CLASSROOM ENGAGEMENT?

Classroom engagement is the active and enthusiastic participation of students in the learning process within a classroom setting. Engaged students are mentally and emotionally invested in their learning, showing interest, attentiveness, and a willingness to interact with the teacher, peers, and the academic content. This active involvement goes beyond passive listening and includes deeper thinking, asking questions, contributing to discussions, completing assignments, and actively seeking to understand the material being taught.

Engaged students are motivated to learn and they demonstrate higher levels of focus, curiosity, and critical thinking. They are more likely to retain information, make connections between concepts, and apply their learning to real-life situations. Classroom engagement is a key indicator of a positive and effective learning environment, as it fosters a sense of ownership and responsibility for learning. This leads to better academic outcomes and a positive overall learning experience. Most of all, kids are happier!

THE IMPORTANCE OF CLASSROOM ENGAGEMENT

Classroom engagement is so important as it plays a vital role in student learning, academic achievement, and overall classroom dynamics. When students are actively engaged in the learning process, they become more motivated, attentive, and focused, leading to several key benefits.

Enhanced Learning and Retention: Engaged students are more likely to absorb and retain information. Active participation helps solidify concepts in their minds, leading to better comprehension and long-term retention.

Increased Academic Achievement: Engaged students perform better academically. They are more likely to complete assignments, participate in class discussions, achieve higher grades, and produce higher quality work that they are proud to show off.

Improved Critical Thinking Skills: Classroom engagement promotes critical thinking, problem-solving, and decision-making skills. Students actively analyze and apply information, fostering a deeper understanding of the content they are learning. Ask a variety of questions ranging from low level simple questions to questions that require deeper thinking and application.

THE IMPORTANCE OF CLASSROOM ENGAGEMENT

Positive Learning Experience: When students are engaged, they enjoy the learning process more, leading to a positive association with school. This positive experience can lead to a lifelong love of learning and maybe even future teachers.

Greater Inclusivity and Equity: Engaging activities can accommodate diverse learning styles and abilities, creating a more inclusive classroom environment. All students, regardless of their strengths or challenges, can participate and contribute. This needs to be a focus from the first day of school so that it's built into your classroom culture.

Building a Supportive Classroom Culture: Engagement fosters a sense of community and collaboration among students. They learn to work well together, support each other, and develop social skills. These skills will benefit them forever.

THE IMPORTANCE OF CLASSROOM ENGAGEMENT

Reduced Behavioral Issues: Engaged students are less likely to be disruptive or disengaged, leading to a more focused and orderly classroom environment. As a teacher myself, I have experienced this first hand, seeing kids thrive in the right environment for them. They feel a sense of belonging and truly enjoying the learning experience. It's not perfect, but the behavior just seems to go away, as crazy as that may sound.

Increased Satisfaction: Teachers experience higher job satisfaction when they see their students actively engaged and excited about learning. It creates a positive and fulfilling learning experience for kids and rewarding teaching experience for adults. Families know when their kids are happy at school because it shows in many ways. Every year, I seem to have a touching story from a family who tells me that their kid "likes school now." I don't think it is a coincidence...it's called CLASSROOM ENGAGEMENT (and relationship building).

Preparation for Real-Life Situations: Engaged learning often involves problem-solving and decision-making activities that mirror real-life situations. This prepares students for future challenges and responsibilities at school and in the real world.

THE IMPORTANCE OF CLASSROOM ENGAGEMENT

Promotes Autonomy and Ownership: Engagement empowers students to take ownership of their learning. They become active participants in the learning process, which fosters self-directed learning. They care about their learning and try harder.

Positive Effects on Well-Being: Engaged students tend to have lower levels of stress and anxiety related to academic tasks. A positive and supportive classroom environment contributes to their overall well-being. When they feel good about what they are working on, they will show pride in their work.

Active Participation and Inquiry: Engagement encourages students to ask questions, seek answers, and explore topics beyond what is covered in the curriculum. It's fun to watch students get excited about topics, wanting to learn more and diving deeper into learning.

Classroom engagement is vital for student success and a positive learning experience. As educators, creating an engaging learning environment should be a priority to ensure that all students have the opportunity to thrive and reach their full potential.

BENEFITS OF CLASSROOM ENGAGEMENT

Increases Motivation: As discussed earlier, kids take accountability for their learning. By introducing elements of competition and reward, students are more motivated to actively participate in their learning.

Encourages Collaboration: Partner, small group, and team-based games foster collaboration and communication among students. Gamification makes learning enjoyable and interactive, capturing students' attention and interest.

Promotes Critical Thinking: Games and gamified activities often require problem-solving and critical thinking skills to succeed. These are important skills to foster at a young age.

Provides Immediate Feedback: Many games and gamified tools offer instant feedback, allowing students to learn from mistakes and make improvements. This is especially true for technology based games.

Builds a Growth Mindset: Games and gamification emphasize effort and improvement, promoting a growth mindset among students. Kids need to experience a growth mindset early in their education.

9

BENEFITS OF CLASSROOM ENGAGEMENT

Happy Students: Students will enjoy school more if they are fully engaged in their learning. It is likely to improve attendance at school.

Increased Socialization: Students will have the opportunity to communicate and interact with each other. Most kids have to learn to communicate, respectively and assertively, with their peers. This is not a skill that all kids have as they enter school.

Lifelong Learning: Increased engagement in the classroom has a positive impact on learning, inspiring a lifelong love of learning and interacting.

INCREASED ENGAGEMENT & CLASSROOM MANAGEMENT

Establish Clear Rules and Procedures: Set clear and consistent expectations from the beginning of the school year. Develop class rules together-kids usually come up with everything you would want to see. The earlier you have this running smoothly, the better off you will be the rest of the year.

Use Positive Reinforcement: Acknowledge and reward positive behavior and active engagement. Offer verbal praise, encouragement, and small incentives to reinforce positive actions. If you use tickets, dollars or class points, this is a great time to use them. You can reward student by student, teams or the whole class.

Create a Respectful and Inclusive Environment: Foster a classroom culture that values and respects each student's contributions. I always make it a point to make sure kids recognize that we are all different, but have so many similarities at the same time. Building respect for one another and showing empathy is key to a positive classroom environment. Encourage students to be inclusive and supportive of all their peers at all times.

INCREASED ENGAGEMENT & CLASSROOM MANAGEMENT

Differentiate Instruction: Accommodate diverse learning styles and abilities by differentiating instruction. Offer varied activities and materials to meet individual needs and interests. All kids do not learn the same way and need various opportunities to show their learning.

Provide Engaging Learning Materials: Use a variety of engaging and interactive learning materials, including games, technology and hands-on activities so that kids don't get bored in class.

Encourage Active Participation: Create a classroom atmosphere where all students feel comfortable participating. Avoid putting students on the spot or making them uncomfortable when they answer questions. I never make kids participate, but eventually they choose to participate if you welcome it. Providing a microphone for kids to share work or introduce themselves makes a huge difference. They feel like celebrities and get a little embarrassed when they use it at first, but t increases participation a great deal.

INCREASED ENGAGEMENT & CLASSROOM MANAGEMENT

Set Clear Learning Objectives: Communicate learning objectives clearly. Try to tie them to the real-world so kids understand. Students are more likely to engage when they understand the relevance of what they are learning. Make sure kids understand the learning objectives and the why.

Allow for Movement and Brain Breaks: Incorporate movement and brain breaks into the daily routine to help students refocus and maintain engagement. This can include simple, quick breaks or going to another location in the room to get materials or supplies.

Provide Timely Feedback: Offer timely and constructive feedback to students on their work and participation. This helps them understand their progress and areas for improvement. This also helps them to feel heard.

INCREASED ENGAGEMENT & CLASSROOM MANAGEMENT

Facilitate Partner, Small Group or Team Activities: Working together with other kids is so important for learning, but also for socialization. Try to use small group activities and discussions to encourage collaboration and interaction among students. Incorporate teacher time, independent time, partner work and technology to accommodate for all kids having a task at hand. Practicing this routine is important so kids know your expectations and learning progresses during small group instruction.

Model Enthusiasm and Interest: Show enthusiasm for the subject matter and learning process. Your passion can be contagious and motivate students to engage more actively. This really has truth. Try showing a lot of interest and excitement. For example, a story about climbing Mount Everest could be a little boring, but it was very fun. Half thought they may want to try it some day, but after I introduced it with such excitement and read with such interest, almost all thought they may try it some day. Likely? Probably not, but I love the fact that they knew it was possible if they chose to. We did a cool black and white mountain art project and writing activity to follow.

14

INCREASED ENGAGEMENT & CLASSROOM MANAGEMENT

Promote Student Voice: Encourage students to share their ideas, opinions, and questions. Create a safe environment where all voices are valued. Offer many different modes where kids can speak because not all kids will be comfortable talking in front of the whole class, at first. It is important that all kids are heard in some fashion, whether it be in small groups, partner talk or teams. If working in teams, try assigning roles so all kids have a task to focus on and all get a chance to participate.

Encourage Reflection: Incorporate reflection activities where students think about their learning experiences and set goals for improvement. It is important for kids to reflect so they can recognize their strengths and what they are proud of. It also reminds them to strive to find improvements they can make in themselves.

Monitor and Adjust: Continuously monitor student engagement and adjust your teaching strategies based on the class responses and needs. Be flexible and willing to try new things. When I learn something new, I want to try it right away. I know if I just write it down, I may never come back to it, so I just go for it.

INCREASED ENGAGEMENT & CLASSROOM MANAGEMENT

Set Realistic Expectations: Set achievable goals and expectations based on the students' abilities and the content being taught. Celebrate small successes along the way and the big successes at the end. This can be at the end of a unit or at the end of project based learning.

Building Relationships: Getting to know your students is the most important key to increasing engagement in the classroom. All of your students need to trust you and know you like (or love) them. They will work harder if they know that, but don't assume they know it.

CREATING A POSITIVE CLASSROOM CULTURE

Building Relationships: Getting to know your students is very important to increasing engagement in the classroom, but promoting relationship building between students is also important. They need to feel comfortable with each other and getting to know one another is a huge part of that comfortability. Let kids interact so they will be more comfortable.

Establish Classroom Norms: Involve students in creating classroom norms that promote cooperation and communication, setting expectations for respectful interaction. Let them be a part of the decision making so they have more invested in respecting the norms.

Celebrating Teamwork: Recognize and celebrate examples of successful cooperation and communication within the classroom. I make a big deal out of small successes!

Community Service Projects: Engage students in community service projects that require cooperation and effective communication with others outside the classroom. This can simply be at school, using efforts to make the school better. A lot of pride is felt when kids come together to make a project come to fruition.

17

BEGINNING OF YEAR ACTIVITIES

Paper Airplane Introductions: Each child writes their name and something they enjoy on a paper airplane. Then, they throw their airplanes into the air and pick up one that lands near them, meeting and introducing the owner.

Skittle Sharing: Ski-tell about yourself is an activity where students get a small cup or bag of skittles. As they choose a color, they share a different facts about themselves based on ideas displayed in front of them.

About Me Activities: You can give questionnaires, host student meet & greets, or get to know you scavenger hunts. Students can also fill out a pennant template and share their favorite items with the class.

Getting to Know the Teacher Activity: Share information about yourself with the class, such as your favorite book, hobbies, or places you've visited. This personal touch helps students connect with you as their teacher. You can also create and give a True False quiz. It's fun to see how many they get right or wrong.

BEGINNING OF YEAR ACTIVITIES

Classroom Tour or Scavenger Hunt: Give students a guided tour of the classroom, highlighting important areas like the reading corner, supplies station, and drinking fountain. You can also give them a list of questions that lead them to explore the room. Students can work together to find the answers, such as "what is on the schedule at 11:30?"or "where is the bathroom pass?" It is fun to customize your own scavenger hunt based on your classroom.

Name Games: Play name games to help everyone in the class learn other names. This can include activities like "Name Bingo" or creating name tags with unique facts about each student. There is a free game called PEER-O on Teachers Pay Teachers that is a fun way for kids to get to know each other, especially for new students.

Classroom Quilt: Create a classroom quilt by having each student decorate fabric or paper square with their name and a drawing that represents them. Assemble the squares to form a quilt that symbolizes the class community.

Don't forget to take a classroom photo!

ICE BREAKERS

Name and Favorite: Have each student introduce themselves by saying their name and sharing their favorite color, food, animal, or hobby. It's a simple way to learn names and interests.

Emoji Emotions: Prepare cards with different emoji faces expressing various emotions. Each student picks a card and shares a time when they felt that emotion.

Interview a Friend: Pair up students and have them interview each other with a set of fun questions you provide. Keep it simple to 5 questions or less so they can switch partners. Later, they introduce their partner to the whole group.

Draw and Share: Give each child a piece of paper and some markers or crayons. Ask them to draw something that represents their favorite hobby or a memorable experience. Afterward, they share their drawing and the story behind it.

ICE BREAKERS

Find a Friend Scavenger Hunt: Create a grid of characteristics or experiences (e.g., has a pet, visited a specific place). Kids mingle and find someone who fits each box, encouraging interactions. There are free versions of these back to school activities on Teachers Pay Teachers.

Mystery Bag: Bring a bag with a few interesting objects inside. Pass the bag around, each student takes an item out and talks about it or shares a story related to the object. Kids can also take a bag home, then bring it back with 5 items that represent them. They get to share the items with the class, like show and tell.

Group Juggle: Have kids stand in a circle. Toss a soft ball or stuffed animal to one student and ask them a simple question (e.g., favorite color). That student, then tosses the ball to someone else, asking a new question or the same question if they can't think of one.

Group Chain: Students work together in teams, making a paper chain from materials you provide. I usually give two 9X12 pieces of construction paper and a roll of masking tape. The team goal is to make the longest paper chain.

ICE BREAKERS FOR OLDER KIDS

Common Interest Challenge: Divide kids into pairs or small groups based on shared interests or hobbies. They discuss their favorite books, movies, games, or any other similar interests. The goal is to find "common ground" with others in the group.

Two Truths and a Dream: Similar to "Two Truths and a Lie," but instead of a lie, each person shares two truths and one dream or aspiration they have for the future.

Two Truths and a Whopper: A humorous twist on "Two Truths and a Lie." Instead of a lie, participants share two true statements and one outrageous or funny statement that sounds like a lie, but is it?

The Playlist Game: Have each kid create a short playlist of three to five songs that represent their personality or current mood. After sharing the playlist, they can explain why they chose those songs.

ICE BREAKERS FOR OLDER KIDS

Historical Time Capsule: Give each participant a blank piece of paper and ask them to draw or write about what they think their life might be like in 10 or 20 years. Share and discuss the predictions.

The Superlative Game: Have kids vote on various superlatives for their peers, such as "Best Sense of Humor," "Most Adventurous," or "Best Cook." Share the results in a lighthearted way. Have LOTS of categories that fit lots of different students.

Sentence Completion: Provide sentence starters like "My favorite memory from last summer was..." or "One thing I'd like to learn more about is..." or "If you could go anywhere in the world, where would you go?" Kids complete the sentences and share their responses.

Emoji Charades: Write down a list of funny or absurd situations on cards, and have participants act them out using only emojis. Others have to guess the situation.

ICE BREAKERS FOR OLDER KIDS

Who Am I?: Prepare name tags for each student with the name of a famous person, a character from a book/movie, or a historical figure. Kids must ask yes-or-no questions to figure out who they are.

Hidden Talents Showcase: Have each student reveal a unique talent or skill they have that others might not know about. It could be anything from a magic trick to rolling their tongue a weird way.

Back to Back Drawing: Pair up students and have them sit back to back. One person describes an image that they are looking at. The other person tries to draw it based on the description. Then, they compare the original image to the drawing.

Mime Time: Create a list of funny and quirky scenarios, and have students or pairs of students take turns miming those situations while others guess what they're acting out. This can be a very funny icebreaker.

ICE BREAKERS FOR OLDER KIDS

Create a Caption: Show students a funny or silly picture. Have them come up with creative and humorous captions for it. Let them work with partners or teams to increase participation.

Fishbowl Follies: Write down funny words or phrases on slips of paper and put them in a fishbowl or basket. Students take turns picking a slip and using that word or phrase to answer questions or describe themselves.

Invent a Silly Greeting: Have students pair up and invent the silliest and most unique greeting they can think of to welcome each other.

Funny Impersonations: Encourage students to do funny impersonations of well-known personalities or characters. It can be anything from movie characters to famous celebrities.

If You Could...: Ask each student to complete the sentence "If you could..." with a fun hypothetical question. For example, "If you could have any superpower, what would it be and why?"

ICE BREAKERS FOR OLDER KIDS

Would You Rather: Have students create their own version of "Would you rather..." questions. Display the questions and let kids pick a side of the room to show their answer. Encourage discussion if you have time. Have students acknowledge other students that have the same interest. Have them greet a classmate with something in common by giving the following directions:

- Shake hands
- Fist Bump
- High Five
- Double High Five
- Ankle Bump
- Bow
- Elbow Bump
- Head Nod
- Salute
- Wave
- Make Up Your Own Handshake

Go Noodle has some fun games that incorporate some of these acknowledgements called "This or That?" and it's free!

WHY GAMES?

Games have a remarkable ability to enhance engagement and motivation in various educational settings, especially the classroom. When used thoughtfully and strategically, games can transform the learning experience and create a positive impact on students. Here's how games can achieve this:

Intrinsic Motivation: Games often tap into students' intrinsic motivation, making the learning process enjoyable and fulfilling. The challenge, competition, and sense of accomplishment in games can be rewarding, motivating students to actively participate. They actually want to participate instead of having to participate or being forced to participate.

Active Learning: Games promote active learning, where students become active participants rather than passive observers. They engage in problem-solving, critical thinking, and decision-making, which leads to a deeper understanding of the content. You can tell when a student is learning actively or sitting back and daydreaming. If you increase engagement, you will definitely see more active learning.

WHY GAMES?

Immediate Feedback: Many games provide instant feedback, allowing students to know immediately how well they are performing. This feedback loop reinforces their learning and encourages them to improve. This ranges from math fluency games with a right or wrong answer to the technology based games that give them feedback as they go or as soon as they have finished the task.

Competition and Collaboration: Games often involve healthy competition, which can spur students to excel and perform their best. Additionally, collaborative games foster teamwork and cooperation, creating a positive social dynamic in the classroom. In a classroom with positive collaboration, it allows for kids to want to work with any other student in the classroom.

Safe Learning Environment: Games provide a safe space for experimentation and exploration. Students can take risks, make mistakes, and learn from them without fear of negative consequences. We always make sure kids know that mistakes help us grow. Games include rules and expectations should be set for kids to play respectfully. If these expectations are set early, it should be. a great school year where kids love working with each other without complaint.

WHY GAMES?

Personalization and Differentiation: Games can be adapted to suit different learning styles and abilities, allowing each student to progress at their own pace and feel a sense of achievement. Students can be grouped in a variety of ways such as by like ability or to mentor and learn from each other.

Engaging Content Delivery: Games have the power to deliver content in an engaging and interactive manner. Complex concepts can be presented in a fun and accessible way, increasing student interest and comprehension. It also increases their buy in for wanting to learn.

Longer Attention Span: Games often captivate student attention for more extended periods compared to traditional teaching methods. They become immersed in the game, leading to improved focus and concentration. Time does fly when you're having fun, it does pass fast when you are immersed in learning games.

Emotional Connection: Games can evoke emotions and create personal connections with the content. When students are emotionally invested, they are more likely to remember and apply what they have learned.

WHY GAMES?

Continual Progression: Many games offer a sense of progression, where students can see their growth and improvement over time. This sense of achievement motivates them to continue learning and mastering new skills.

Engaging Assessment: Games can be used as assessment tools, providing an engaging and interactive way to gauge students' understanding and learning progress. Put aside that paper, pencil test and let the auto grading save you some time.

Reduction of Anxiety: Games can help reduce anxiety related to learning, especially in subjects that students find challenging. The gamified environment promotes a positive attitude toward learning.

When integrating games into the classroom, it's essential to align them with specific learning objectives and curricular goals. Strategic use of games alongside traditional teaching methods can create a balanced and effective learning experience that maximizes engagement and motivation among students.

GAMIFICATION IN THE CLASSROOM

Gamification is applying a game concept to your classroom as an overall theme. Students get excited and have a buy in when presented with a theme. Gamified themes can be based on board games, such as Monopoly to video games, such as Minecraft. It can also be based on a concept or place.

Project based learning is another way to make a classroom feel gamified, especially when you add competition into play. For example, students design and plan for their own food truck through writing. Then, they get to construct a food truck using the cutest template. They make a paper menu or design one on Canva.com, which sits like a billboard by the small constructed food truck. They end with a competition and kids from the adjacent class votes, while we vote on their trucks. The kids are proud to show off their work.

GAMIFICATION IN THE CLASSROOM

Points and Badges System: Implement a points-based system where students earn points for completing assignments, participating in discussions, helping their peers, or exhibiting positive behavior. Offer badges or rewards for reaching specific milestones, such as "Top Contributor," "Perfect Attendance" or "Lifesaver."

Leaderboards: Create a digital leaderboard that displays the top-performing students based on their points or achievements. Make sure to have lots of categories where all kids can find success. You can also create a leaderboard on a large poster. This fosters healthy competition and encourages students to strive for excellence.

Educational Games: Integrate educational games and quizzes into the curriculum that reinforce the concepts being taught. These games can be played individually or in teams, and they can cover various subjects and topics. Read further for lots of game ideas.

GAMIFICATION IN THE CLASSROOM

Quest-Based Learning: Frame the learning process as a quest, where students embark on a journey to achieve specific learning objectives. As they progress, they unlock new challenges and gain rewards.

Storytelling and Narrative: Integrate storytelling and narrative elements into lessons to make them more engaging and relatable to students. This could involve creating stories with characters facing challenges related to the subject matter.

Virtual Field Trips: Take students on virtual field trips using augmented reality (AR) or virtual reality (VR) technology. This gives them the opportunity to explore places they might not otherwise be able to visit. No VR? That's ok, see the Virtual Field Trip Ideas chapter later in this book for a vast list of ideas worth trying.

Class-wide Collaborative Challenges: Set goals for the entire class to work together towards achieving. For example, if the class reads a certain number of books collectively, they earn a reward such as a pizza party or extra recess.

GROUP GAMES

Classroom Bingo: Create bingo cards with different concepts or terms related to the lesson. As you cover the material, students mark off the squares until someone gets a bingo. You can also play Multiplication Bingo or Word Bingo. Whatever you may have, play it!

Charades: Similar to Pictionary, but instead of drawing, students act out words or phrases related to the lesson for their teams to guess. Vocabulary words are fun to act out on a regular basis. It doesn't take any prep and kids love to participate.

GROUP GAMES

Tic-Tac-Toe: Create a tic-tac-toe grid on the board with questions or tasks related to the lesson. Divide the class into two teams and take turns asking questions. Teams earn a spot on the board for each correct answer. The first team to get three in a row wins.

Memory Game: Prepare a tray with several items related to the lesson. Show it to the class for a brief period, then cover the tray and have students write down or discuss as many items as they can remember and how they relate to the lesson.

PARTNER GAMES

Round Robin Brainstorming: Have students sit in a circle. Pose a question related to the topic, each student takes turns providing one answer or idea until everyone has participated.

Guess Who?: Prepare cards with names of historical figures, scientists, characters, or any relevant personalities from the subject you're teaching. Students take turns asking yes-or-no questions to guess who is written on their card.

Jigsaw Puzzle: Prepare jigsaw puzzle pieces with questions, answers, or parts of a larger image related to the lesson. Students work together to solve the puzzle while discussing the content.

COLLABORATIVE & TEAM BUILDING GAMES

Team Building Towers: Provide each team with supplies like index cards, straws, and tape. Teams must work together to build the tallest tower using the materials provided.

Spider Web: Create a "spider web" using yarn or string between objects in the room. Students must navigate through the web without touching it, helping each other to find the best path. You can have students retrieve items within the web, which adds an extra challenge.

Group Drawing: Divide students into groups and give each group a large piece of paper. One student starts drawing a picture, then passes it to the next person, who adds to it, and so on, until the drawing is complete. Let groups share with the rest of the class.

Group Storytelling: Students sit in a circle, each person takes turns adding a sentence to a collaborative story. The story continues until everyone has had a chance to contribute.

COLLABORATIVE & TEAM BUILDING GAMES

Cup Stack Challenge: Provide each team with a set of cups. The teams must work together to stack the cups in a specific pattern or tower within a time limit. You can reuse the cups every year or use them for something else.

Cross the River: Set up an imaginary "river" using hula hoops or pieces of paper. Students must work together to cross the river without touching the "water."

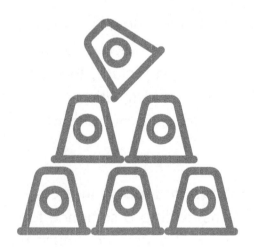

TEAM CHALLENGES & COMPETITIONS

Trivia Challenge: Host a trivia competition with teams competing to answer questions on various topics related to the curriculum. The trivia can be on any topic or subject and works well to reinforce concepts.

STEM Challenges: Present science, technology, engineering, and math challenges that require teams to design and build solutions to specific problems. Add art to make it a STEAM challenge. My favorite is making Native American shelters.

Debate Competition: Organize a debate competition on relevant and thought-provoking topics, where teams argue their viewpoints. Topics can also be simple like "what is the best class pet?" This is fun way to introduce persuasive writing.

Spelling Bee: Conduct a spelling bee competition with teams representing their classes or groups. Consider taking spelling bee school wide or maybe your school and/or district already has a spelling bee in place. If so, take advantage of it because a lot of kids still love the old fashioned spelling bee.

TEAM CHALLENGES & COMPETITIONS

Book Trivia Bowl or Battle of the Books: Have teams compete in a trivia bowl based on books they've read or from an assigned book list. A battle encourages reading comprehension and knowledge. This activity can be quite challenging, but even better, kids are reading!

Art Competition: Organize an art competition where teams create artwork based on a specific theme or technique. Not a great artist, no problem! Art for Kids Hub on YouTube has so many different step by step choices.

Escape Room Race: Set up multiple mini escape room challenges, and have teams race against the clock to solve them.

Entrepreneurship Challenge: Have teams create and present business plans for innovative products or services. I love incorporating entrepreneurship when reading about Thomas Edison. Students think about what has been invented and what they would like to see invented. This is a very creative project that doesn't take much preparation.

NEWS REPORTING

Reporting News: Have students write a news script, practice it and report back to the class. Anything worth sharing is worth reporting. This can be a school event or classroom project. Provide a microphone, it is well worth the investment.

Reporting News in a Video: Record the news story on video, either with classroom technology or your cell phone. You can embed videos into a news background template. I recommend using Canva.com for video templates that are ready to go with professional backgrounds and music.

Other Roles: Interviewing, clacking a movie set clacker and holding the script on a clipboard are other roles that give students opportunities to be involved. I invested in a black landscape clipboard to hold the script and movie set clacker. Kids beg to participate in some capacity.

This has been a very positive experience in my classroom and all kids were involved in the news reporting process. I definitely plan to carry on the tradition every year.

FUN GAMES

Musical Chairs (with a Twist): Place learning-related questions or flashcards on the chairs. When the music stops, students sit on a chair and answer the question they find. You can continue the game until there is a winner, but every time the music stops, read a new card or cards.

Snowball Fight: Each student writes a response to a question on a piece of paper, crumples it into a "snowball," and tosses it around the room. Afterward, students pick up a snowball, read the response, and share it with their partner. Set ground rules prior to playing this game.

Rock-Paper-Scissors Showdown or Tournament: Divide the class into pairs for a quick rock-paper-scissors tournament or create a bracket. Have 2 kids compete, the winner moves forward on the bracket. Keep playing until you have the last 2 students standing. This is a fun game that doesn't take any preparation and it goes quicker than you think.

Tongue Twister Challenge: Divide the class into teams and give each team a set of tongue twisters to practice and recite. The team that can say the tongue twisters accurately and quickly wins.

FUN GAMES

Simon Says: Play a variation of "Simon Says" with educational commands related to the lesson. For example, "Simon says clap your hands if 2+2 equals 4" or "Simon says clap your hands if whales migrate."

Roll the Dice Review: Assign different review questions to each number on a dice. Students take turns rolling the dice and answering the corresponding question.

SCAVENGER HUNT GAMES

Math Hunt: Create a list of math problems or equations related to the current lesson. Hide the questions around the classroom, students must find and solve each problem. You can even just display problems around the room and solve the problems, scoot style.

Word Wall Scavenger Hunt: If you have a word wall with vocabulary words related to the subject, create clues for each word and have students find and match the words to the clues. This can be really fun and it helps students remember the meaning of the words.

Book Hunt: Place various books around the classroom. Give students a list of clues or descriptions of books they need to find, read, or summarize. Be sure to give enough time.

Geography Challenge: Hide small flags or pictures representing different countries around the classroom. Students find the flags and identify the countries on a map. Use class Atlas books if available.

SCAVENGER HUNT GAMES

Parts of Speech Hunt: Create cards with different words around the room. Students sort the words into categories like nouns, verbs, adjectives, etc. This really helps kids to remember the parts of speech if they still need practice with this skill.

Coding Hunt: Hide coding-related symbols or cards around the classroom. Students find the symbols and try to decode or create a simple program with the symbols they collected. You can also use symbols for numbers and they have to decode the message prior to solving the problem.

Teamwork Hunt: Divide the class into teams and provide each team with a set of clues. Each clue leads to the next one until they find a hidden treasure or a reward.

Nature Hunt (Outside): This is a fun activity to do in the fall when kids are spending a lot of time back in the classroom. It is a nice change to go outside for a scavenger hunt and a good time to reinforce outside rules.

QUIET GAMES

Silent Ball: Students stand around the room in a circle. One student starts with a soft foam ball. Students continue to throw the ball to a new student. If students drop the ball on a good toss, they are out. If students talk or laugh, they are also out. It is surprisingly QUIET.

Quiet Ball: Students go around a circle asking a question. Then, they toss the ball to another student. The students must answer the question quietly or in a low tone.

Graveyard: Students lay on the floor and act like they are dead in graveyard. I know it sounds morbid, but they love this game. Select a couple students to go around the room trying to get students to laugh, but those students also have to stay silent.

Uno Challenge: Hold an Uno challenge, but the added rule is...kids can't talk!

INCORPORATING TECHNOLOGY

Quiz Based Review Games that do not require paid subscriptions:

Quizlet Live: Quizlet Live is a team-based game that encourages collaboration and competition. It uses Quizlet flashcard sets to create quiz questions and students work together in teams to answer correctly.

Blooket: "Level up classroom engagement" is Blooket's motto. Students love to create their own "Blook" and play educational games that don't feel educational.

Quizizz: Quizizz offers customizable quizzes and games with competitive elements to engage students in the learning process.

Gimkit: A game-based learning platform that combines quiz and gaming elements, allowing students to earn in-game currency and upgrades.

Nearpod: You can assign relevant lessons and check progress. Kids like this platform because they can work at their own pace and are provided with immediate feedback.

TECHNOLOGY CONT.

Kahoot!: Kahoot! is an interactive quiz-based game that students can play using tablets or computers. You can create your own quizzes or use existing quizzes on the platform. Kahoot has a huge library of games to choose from in all subjects and grade levels. The free version provides everything to need. It's competitive for kids and can be a great way to review or reinforce concepts. In addition, you can even let kids play individually.

There are a a couple resources to support writing that are not free, but they are worth mentioning:

Night Zookeeper: A fun game based program that has many different skills and lessons, which can be assigned by the teacher. Kids like it because it has an illustrating feature to draw characters, but I love it because it helps with spelling, punctuation and grammar.

Pixton: Students can create graphic novels, comic style, with this app. They create their avatar and start creating stories, mostly with dialogue. Kids even love creating stories together.

INCORPORATING TECHNOLOGY

More Educational Apps you can use for free:

Spelling City: You can load lists with your current phonics skill or vocabulary words. Students can choose from free games with your customized list.

Getepic: This reading platform is loaded with differentiated reading options from picture books to chapter books, fiction and non-fiction. Students can choose audio books or read-to-me books. The platform has videos that can be turned off by the teacher.

Prodigy: This is a math-based game and english is also available. Students love playing on this platform because they can find their classmates and have a math battle with them. It gets quite competitive and they look forward to playing again.

99math: This platform allows kids to work on their own path or teachers can lead sessions for the whole class to play together. Logging in is easy for students and they love the timed and competitive nature of this game. It gives lots of awards at the end including "Most Improved" and "Most Accurate."

INCORPORATING TECHNOLOGY

Canva: Students can extend learning in so many ways using Canva.com, a digital creation platform. You can teach students to make a poster, slideshow or video with animation, all related to their learning. They can demonstrate their knowledge while learning new digital creation skills. It is very engaging and they can build on what they learn all year long. Kids love the opportunity to use technology, especially Canva.com.

Google Classroom: This is a perfect app that allows you to communicate with your students and provide links that they may need. You can also take a poll or ask a question through the platform. It is user friendly for teachers to set up and students to use.

Seesaw: A student-driven digital portfolio platform that allows younger students to document and share their learning journey with teachers and families.

Escape Rooms: Design an escape room-style activity where students have to solve puzzles or answer questions correctly to "escape." This can be done physically or digitally using breakout rooms or online tools.

INCORPORATING TECHNOLOGY

Breakout EDU: An immersive learning platform that offers digital escape room experiences where students work collaboratively to solve puzzles and complete challenges. Keep the teacher version open to help you through the challenge as the clues can be quite tricky.

Flipgrid or Flip: A video discussion platform that encourages student voice and collaboration through short video responses to prompts or questions. Students love to record themselves, but have to understand that their peers will see the videos in the same feed. You can ask a question or provide a prompt related to their learning and limit the time they have to record. It is a great way to practice public speaking.

Pear Deck: Flashcard Factory in Pear Deck is a fun and interactive vocabulary technology based game. Partners work together, one partner uses the word in a sentence while the other draws a picture to match the word. Then, they switch roles and the class reviews the flashcards together, giving a thumbs up or thumbs down.

INCORPORATING TECHNOLOGY

Wheel of Names: A tool that randomly selects student names for class participation, making it more engaging and equitable. You can really use it for anything, even rewards. If students get their i-Ready minutes for the week, their name goes on the wheel for a chance to win a prize. I think that is the only reason some of my students look forward to i-Ready.

Padlet: An online collaborative tool that allows students to contribute text, images, and videos to a shared digital wall, promoting creativity and collaboration. Kids get tired of the old Monday morning weekend news so give kids the opportunity to write about their weekend digitally on a Padlet wall. It feels like social media because they get to "like" posts from their peers. It only includes posts from our class.

Plickers: A tool that combines paper cards with QR codes and a smartphone to collect real-time responses from students during polls or quizzes.

Mystery Science: You can get mini lessons without having a membership and if you provide 5 email referrals, then you can unlock all of the mini Mystery Science lessons.

ACTIVITIES TO INCREASE ENGAGEMENT

Classroom Olympics: Organize a series of mini-games or challenges related to the subject matter. Students compete individually or in teams, earning points for their achievements.

Community Model: Set your class up like a city, with appointed officials and jobs. Students learn about how a city works and how to manage money. Use money for kids to earn and also pay for necessary expenses. Money leftover? Rewards are in order! They don't have to be material rewards.

Escape Room: Design an escape room-style activity where students have to solve puzzles or answer questions correctly to "escape." This can be done physically or digitally using breakout rooms or online tools. These are fun and worth the time to prepare if you have the time to devote to it.

Stand Up-Sit Down Quiz: Ask true/false or multiple-choice questions. Students stand up if they think the answer is true or sit down if they believe it is false. This is a good informal way to assess understanding.

ACTIVITIES TO INCREASE ENGAGEMENT

Trashketball: Create a makeshift basketball hoop in the classroom using a trash can or bucket, and assign point values to different types of questions (easy, medium, hard). Divide the class into teams, and when a team answers a question correctly, they get a chance to shoot a paper ball into the hoop for extra points. The orange buckets from Home Depot are a fun alternative to trash cans, but a small basketball hoop is even better.

Bean Bag Toss: Label different learning concepts on the floor with point values. Students toss bean bags onto the labeled areas and answer questions related to the concept they hit. Keep track of points to determine the winning team. You can even put numbers on the floor and kids have to add the points to find out who wins.

Quiz-Quiz-Trade: Each student prepares a question on an index card. They pair up, quiz each other, then trade cards and find new partners to repeat the process.

Speed Debates: Divide the class into two groups and assign each group a different topic to debate. Set a time limit for each debate to keep the pace fast and engaging.

ACTIVITIES TO INCREASE ENGAGEMENT

Gallery Walk: Post different materials or questions around the classroom on large sheets of paper. Divide students into small groups and have them rotate around the room, discussing and responding to the prompts on each sheet. Give them a chance to discuss and share after coming together as a group. This is even good for morning work. Kids love this activity because they get up and move around.

Sentence Relay: Divide the class into teams. Provide each team with a sentence related to the lesson, cut into words. Students race to rearrange the words and form the correct sentence. Make the sentences long enough to provide a challenge.

Whiteboard or Slideshow Races: Divide the class into teams. Show a question or prompt on the whiteboard. The first team to write or answer correctly wins a point. This can be used for any subject or concept.

Four Corners Digital Slide Show: Students are shown 4 pictures and have to choose a corner of the room based on the number on the slide. They love this game and are are constantly moving.

HANDS ON OPPORTUNITIES

It is important to provide hands on opportunities whenever possible. It gets kids excited about learning so I try to incorporate something hands on each week. If you are reading a particular story, how can you pull in art or a STEM activity? If learning a new math concept, how can you provide a hands on learning experience by adding a game or something else?

Try to incorporate activities cross-curricular so you can cover more content and spread the theme for students to have overall buy in to working hard. It helps deepen understanding of the concept being taught. Hands on activities can be offered at the end of a weekly unit so kids are sure to get their work done. They don't want to miss the hands on activity!

MATH GAMES

Math Basketball: Set up a mini basketball hoop in the classroom. Each time a student answers a math question correctly, they get a chance to shoot a small foam ball into the hoop.

Steve Wyborney Number Sense: Games include Esti-Mysteries that focus on helping kids understand number sense, similar to practicing the alphabet in reading. We use white boards and kids write answers. They are constantly showing me their predictions.

Math Jeopardy: Create a Jeopardy-style game where students answer math questions of varying difficulty to earn points. You can find free templates from Matt at Ditch That Textbook and can customize them with any content.

Math Relay Races: Divide students into teams and have them solve math problems in a relay race format. You can have teams solving problems on the front active board or white board. They rotate as each student solves a problem. First team to have all the answers correct, wins. This is highly competitive, but kids love the excitement of it.

MATH GAMES

Math Bingo: Play bingo using math problems. Students mark the answers on their bingo cards. They can practice addition, subtraction, multiplication, division or other skills such as place value or fractions.

Math Puzzles: Provide math puzzles like Sudoku or logic puzzles that challenge problem-solving skills.

Math Board Games: Use board games with a math twist, such as "Mathopoly" (Math Monopoly) or "Fraction War" (using playing cards). Using playing cards for simple fluency of addition and multiplication is a great no prep game that kids ask to play. They love the simple game of war and are strengthening math fluency at the same time.

Math Scavenger Hunt: Hide math problems or equations around the classroom or school. Students find the problems and solve them. I keep a classroom set of clipboards for tasks like this.

Math Tic-Tac-Toe: Play a variation of tic-tac-toe where students must solve math problems to claim a spot on the board.

MATH GAMES

Math Karaoke: Create math-related songs or raps and have students perform them to reinforce math concepts.

Math Songs on YouTube: Check out math songs on YouTube, such as the "Sergeant Seven" multiplication song. Kids love this song and it really sticks in your head. They learn the multiples in a fun, engaging way. It may be one of your favorites too.

Math Memory Match: Create pairs of cards with math problems and solutions. Students flip the cards to find matches.

Math Relay Drawing: Students solve math problems and communicate the answer to a teammate who then draws a portion of a picture based on the answer.

Math Simon Says: Play "Math Simon Says" with math actions, such as "Simon says, add 10 to your current number."

MATH GAMES

Math Basketball: Set up a mini basketball hoop and have students solve math problems to earn shots at the hoop. Using buckets and foam balls is a great way to incorporate basketball into math. We played fraction basketball and it was a big hit. How many shots made out of how many shots taken. For example, you made 4 out of 8 shots, 4/8 or 1/2 of your shots.

Math Dice Games: Roll dice and use the numbers to create math equations or solve problems.

Math Spinners: Use spinners to generate random numbers or math operations for problem-solving. A set of classroom spinners is well worth the investment. I have spinner games that students can choose if done with their work. If you are on a tight budget, kids can use the pencil tip with paperclip method.

Math Challenge Cards: Provide students with math challenge cards of varying difficulty levels. Let them work independently or in groups. Kids actually still love testing each other with flash cards.

READING GAMES

Sight Word Bingo: Create bingo cards with sight or vocabulary words related to the lesson. Students mark off the words as you call them out.

Alphabet Relay Race: Divide the class into teams. Each team races to find objects around the room that start with each letter of the alphabet related to the lesson. Make sure they put the items back as you play.

Vocabulary Relay Race: Divide the class into teams. Each team races to find objects around the room that represents a vocabulary word related to the lesson. For example, rough, fine or rugged. Ready, set, go!

Reading Challenges: Create reading challenges with rewards or incentives to motivate students to read more books.

Reading Buddies: Let students bring a reading buddy from home such as a squish mallow or stuffed animal. You can arrange with another class, younger or older, to read with students in a common area, in one of the classrooms or split the classes half and half.

INCREASING ENGAGEMENT IN READING

Novel Effect: This is a fun app that plays sound out loud through a bluetooth speaker as you read. There is a trial offer, but then you do have to pay to keep it. Our school librarian keeps her subscription active and loves using it when she reads to classes.

Choice of Reading Material: Allow students to choose books and reading materials that interest them. Offer a variety of genres and topics to cater to diverse interests.

Book Clubs or Reading Circles: Organize book clubs or reading circles where students can discuss books they are reading and share their thoughts with peers.

Classroom Reading Buddies: Pair students up as reading buddies in the classroom, where they take turns reading to each other and discussing the story.

INCREASING ENGAGEMENT IN READING

Author Visits or Virtual Read-Aloud Sessions: Invite authors to visit the classroom or conduct virtual read-aloud sessions to make reading more exciting and personal. We had the most amazing author visit at our school! Daryl Cobb incorporated music, reading and storytelling into his visit. He signed books made especially for our school. All the kids were completely engaged the whole time.

Guest Readers: Invite guest readers, such as parents, community members, local authors or older students, to read to the class.

Reader's Theater: Perform reader's theater scripts based on books, allowing students to act out characters and scenes. You can find prepared reader's theater scripts on Teachers Pay Teachers or you can easily make one yourself just by following the storyline.

Book Reviews: Have students write book reviews or create book recommendation posters to share with their classmates. Encourage students to learn about or write to authors.

INCREASING ENGAGEMENT IN READING

Literature Circles: Form literature circles where students read the same book and engage in small-group discussions with assigned roles or turns. Use this especially when you are reading a story with parts.

Interactive Read Aloud: Engage students during read-aloud sessions by asking questions, making predictions, and discussing the story together.

Reading Games and Quizzes: Introduce interactive reading games and quizzes related to the books students are reading.

Book Trailers: Have students create book trailers or short videos to promote their favorite books to others. I recommend Canva.com for this project. If your school does not have educator accounts for you, then you can sign up for a free account using your Google account and your students can as well.

Reading Incentive Programs: Implement school-wide or class-level reading incentive programs to reward students for their reading efforts.

INCREASING ENGAGEMENT IN READING

D.E.A.R. Time: Designate time for Drop Everything and Read (D.E.A.R.) sessions where students can choose a book to read silently. Give time for students to increase stamina. This ends up being a favorite, peaceful part of the day for the students and the teacher.

Reading Corner or Library: Create a cozy reading corner in the classroom or classroom library to make reading inviting and comfortable. I LOVE my classroom library because it offers a large variety of books that kids want to read. It also has bean bag chairs, scoop chairs and a carpet. Kids love it too.

Family Involvement: Involve families in reading activities by sending home book recommendations or having family reading nights. My school participates in One School, One Book, which is a program that provides books and resources for the entire school population. The book is read on the same schedule and it encourages family reading at home.

WRITING GAMES

Interactive Storytelling: Have students sit in a circle. The first student starts a story with one sentence. Then, each student adds one sentence to continue the story, incorporating lesson-related concepts.

Partner Writing: Let students brainstorm and write together, either writing the same story, very similar stories, or taking turns writing sentences.

Group Writing: Have the entire class pass around a story, adding to it as is passed from student to student. It is fun to see how the story turns out and it is not usually what you expect.

Word Games: Engage students in word games like Scrabble, Boggle, or crossword puzzles to build vocabulary and wordplay skills.

What Am I Animal Games: Students choose an animal, write clues and call on classmates to guess what it is. If you start one kid sharing, you may just have all kids sharing by the end of the game.

Scan the QR Code for a FREE download of this game!

WRITING ACTIVITIES

Journaling: Encourage daily or weekly journaling on topics of students' choice. Allow them to write about their experiences, thoughts, and feelings. Let them make up stories too. Rotate through the different genres of writing so students get a taste of the different types. This way, they can figure out which one they like the best. Many times, kids are still trying to figure out writing and what they like, partly due to lack of exposure to all the different types of writing.

Writing Prompts: Provide interesting and thought-provoking writing prompts that stimulate creativity and critical thinking. They can be totally random after playing a song or they can be related to what you are learning in the classroom.

Picture-Based Writing: Show students a captivating image or illustration and have them write a story or descriptive paragraph inspired by it. Focusing on a current event is another way to incorporate writing and discussion into the classroom. You can also show a humorous picture or short clip with a prompt as another engaging hook for writing.

WRITING ACTIVITIES

Creative Writing Workshops: Conduct creative writing workshops to explore different genres like poetry, short stories, and plays. You can do this in your classroom or invite authors and local librarians to visit.

Collaborative Writing: Have students work in pairs or small groups to create collaborative stories or pieces of writing. Students love the opportunity to brainstorm and write together.

Character Development: Ask students to develop in-depth characters and write stories or dialogues based on those characters. It is a fun way to start writing and helps to remove writers block.

Real-World Writing: Connect writing to real-world scenarios, such as writing persuasive letters, creating advertisements, or composing emails.

Writing Contests: Participate in writing contests or organize classroom writing competitions to motivate students.

Sharing: Don't miss the opportunity to allow for sharing and the celebration of writing.

WRITING ACTIVITIES

Create Comic Strips: Let students create comic strips to tell stories or convey messages creatively. They get to illustrate in boxes just like the graphic novels that they love to read.

Writing Center: Set up a writing center in the classroom with writing materials and ideas to encourage spontaneous writing. Set boundaries so students know when it is appropriate to dive in.

Letter Writing: Have students write letters to themselves, family members, future students, or even fictional characters.

Postcard Writing: Have students write postcards to send home to families. They can draw a picture on the front of a blank postcard and write a message on the back. There are free templates you can download on Teachers Pay Teachers. Students learn how to address postcards and put stamps on them for the mail carrier. Kids get super excited to mail actual postcards home. They get equally excited to take a stamped postcard home (addressed to the school) and learn how to mail it back. It's the best homework!

WRITING ACTIVITIES

Publish a Book: We self published a book because it was more affordable for all kids to obtain the books that they were a part of writing. Our class wrote a book titled "Things Third Graders REALLY Love" and they are proud authors! They also illustrated their page. All students got a copy of the book and we had a signing party. There are publishing companies that will send you a publishing kit for free, but the students will have to purchase the books at retail price.

Publishing Parties: Celebrate student writing samples by organizing publishing parties. Students can display and share their work with an audience or display it for a gallery walk.

Use a Mentor Text: Pencils on Strike and Chairs on Strike are great texts to introduce persuasive writing. There are so many opportunities to incorporate writing into the text you are reading with the class. The pencils or chairs actually go on strike and students have to persuade them to come back. Allow students to write their own stories; Books on Strike! Chromebooks on Strike! Homework on Strike! Oh my!

STRATEGIES TO INCREASE ENGAGEMENT

Community Circle or Meeting: Start the day with a meeting or fit it in any time throughout the day. Discuss what is going well and problem solve what is not. It gives your students a chance to continue to get to know each other. This can be a game changer and change the mood in your classroom.

Points and Rewards: Assign points to students for completing tasks, participating in discussions, or achieving learning goals. Accumulated points can be used to unlock rewards or privileges.

Classroom Money System: Award dollars to students for completing tasks, participating in discussions, or achieving learning goals. Even recognize when students are helpful or complete classroom jobs. Accumulated dollars can be spent on whatever you choose to let them buy. There are many options for non-material rewards such as using a special chair for the day, eating lunch in class, being the teacher helper, 10 minutes of free time, indoor recess coupons, and so much more.

STRATEGIES TO INCREASE ENGAGEMENT

Simulation Games: Incorporate simulation games related to real-life scenarios, where students can make decisions and see the consequences of their choices.

Homework Lottery: This is a game changer! My students went from avoiding homework to asking for it. A homework lottery is a grid with numbers and allows the kids to put their name on a number as they complete homework. When the board is full, we do a drawing. There can be lots of prizes or just one.

Whoa! Lottery: This can work for wow moments as well. If a student does outstanding work, goes above and beyond, or for any other WHOA! moment, let them put their name on a square. You can create a Bingo system to pull the numbers once it is filled up.

Quick Fire Questions: Pose quick and fun questions to the class, allowing each student to answer, one after the other, in rapid succession.

PARTNER TALK STRATEGIES

Think-Pair-Share: Pose a question or problem to the whole class. Give students a moment to think individually, then have them pair up to discuss their thoughts. Give both students an equal chance to talk. Finally, ask a few pairs to share their ideas with the whole class.

Numbered Heads Together: Assign numbers to each student in a group. Pose a question and students work together to come up with an answer. Then, call out a number, and the students with that number from each group share their group's response.

Jigsaw Activity: Divide a larger topic or reading material into sections. Have students form expert groups, where each group studies a specific section. Then, reorganize the groups so that each new group has one "expert" from each section. Students share their expertise with their new group. The students learn about the whole concept after studying just a small part of it.

Talking Chips or Talking Sticks: Students take turn talking. Whoever has the chip or stick, talks, simple as that.

PARTNER TALK STRATEGIES

Inside-Outside Circle: Form two circles with one circle of students facing outward and the other circle facing inward. Students pair up and discuss a topic. After a designated time, one circle rotates, and they discuss with a new partner.

Lines of Communication: Form two lines facing each other. Students should be across from a partner. If uneven, you can partner up or give one student a pass. Students pair up and discuss a topic or answer a question. After a designated time, one line moves down one student, and they discuss with a new partner. Once this strategy is taught, it is easy to incorporate without much effort.

First, Line 1 speaks, then Line 2 speaks

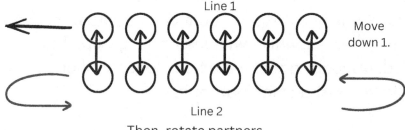

Then, rotate partners.,

Peer Teaching: Assign topics to pairs of students and have them prepare short presentations to teach the rest of the class.

GROUP PROBLEM SOLVING ACTIVITIES

Marshmallow Tower: Provide each group with marshmallows and spaghetti or toothpicks. It is also fun to provide different sizes of marshmallows. The objective is to build the tallest freestanding tower using the materials within a given time limit. Make sure you let kids know when time is ticking down.

Building Bridges: Using limited materials like straws, tape, and paper, challenge groups to build the strongest bridge that can support a specific weight. They can test it using small objects in the classroom.

Foil Boats: Give each student a piece of foil (12"X12"). Ask them to construct a boat that can float in water and hold pennies. It gets competitive to see which boat can hold the most pennies.

Minefield: Set up an obstacle course with various objects on the floor. Blindfolded team members must navigate through the "minefield" with the guidance of their teammates' verbal instructions. This is quite challenging and forces students to communicate.

GROUP PROBLEM SOLVING ACTIVITIES

The Egg Drop Challenge: Students must design and build a contraption to protect a raw egg from breaking when dropped from a height.

Invention Convention: Each group comes up with a creative invention to solve a real-world problem and presents it to the class. This is fun to pair with anything to do with inventions.

Save Fred: Place a gummy worm (Fred) inside and under a clear plastic cup. Place a gummy lifesaver on top of the cup (boat). Give students 2 paperclips that they can use to save Fred. He needs to get back in his boat with his lifesaving vest on. Students must figure out how to get the lifesaver on the gummy worm (Fred) and get Fred into the cup (boat).

EASY BRAIN BREAKS

Brain Teasers on YouTube: Type "brain teasers for kids" into YouTube and you will have a variety to choose from. Make sure you watch them first to make sure they are appropriate for kids and it's what you are looking for.

Go Noodle: There are so many different brain breaks, low energy to high energy for all elementary age kids.

Stretching Exercises: Guide students through simple stretching exercises like reaching for the sky, touching their toes, or doing shoulder rolls.

Dance Party: Play a favorite song and let students dance around for a minute or two.

Karaoke: Kids love singing and they are actually reading when doing karaoke.

Breathing Exercises: Teach students deep breathing techniques, such as "Take 5 Breaths" (inhale for a count of 5, exhale for a count of 5). You can also try box breathing where students breathe in and out as they draw each sides of the box. Just make sure to switch it up and try different kinds of breathing techniques.

EASY BRAIN BREAKS

Quick Draw: Give students a prompt to draw something related to the lesson in 30 seconds or less. Let them share if you have time.

Color Hunt: Ask students to find and name objects of a particular color in the classroom. They don't even need to touch the object.

Word Association: Say a word and have students quickly shout out related words.

Tongue Twisters: Have students try saying fun and challenging tongue twisters together.

Counting Claps: Have students stand up and clap their hands a certain number of times, counting aloud together. Try clapping different patterns and have them copy.

EASY BRAIN BREAKS

One-Minute Challenges: Set a timer for one minute and challenge students to see how many jumping jacks, high knees, or arm circles they can do in that time. You can use any exercises you would like. You can even use it for non-exercise tasks. Online Stopwatch has some fun timers that make timing more fun.

Quick Riddles: Pose simple riddles for students to solve in a short amount of time. Knock, Knock jokes are always a quick way to engage kids.

Funny Faces: Have students make silly or exaggerated facial expressions to make each other laugh.

Name Game Rhymes: Go around the room and have each student say their name with a rhyming word or phrase (e.g., "Sara from afar," "Alex with the hex"). This gets kids laughing for sure.

VIRTUAL FIELD TRIP IDEAS

California PORTS Program: Sign up to receive notifications for field trip opportunities from the California State Parks, many of which, are online or web based. They offer live field trips that are actual guided trips with a real park ranger. As a teacher from Oregon I was able to to sign up as a non-resident. I have personally taken my class to the Pacific Ocean on a kayak, Sequoia National Park, North Coast Redwoods, Point Lobos State Park, Hearst Castle and La Purisima Mission all hosted by park rangers.

Museums and Art Galleries: Visit famous museums virtually, such as The Louvre in Paris, the British Museum in London, or the Smithsonian National Museum of Natural History in Washington, D.C. Discover famous artworks in virtual art galleries, like the Van Gogh Museum in Amsterdam.

VIRTUAL FIELD TRIP IDEAS

Space Exploration: Explore space through virtual tours of the International Space Station or the surface of Mars. Live cams and books read by astronauts are available on YouTube.

National Parks: Virtually visit stunning national parks like Yellowstone, Grand Canyon, or Banff National Park. Google Maps provides a great view of these parks and kids can explore at their own pace if they have devices. If not, it's fun to explore as a group.

Aquariums: Take a virtual tour of aquariums to discover marine life and underwater ecosystems. Various live cams are also available at many aquariums.

Historical Sites: Explore historical sites like the Pyramids of Giza in Egypt, the Colosseum in Rome, or Machu Picchu in Peru, all digitally.

VIRTUAL FIELD TRIP IDEAS

Ride on a Roller Coaster: You can ride on Space Mountain and take 360 virtual roller coaster rides. These videos are available on YouTube. You can also see Disneyland in Paris.

Virtual Farm Tours: Discover farming practices and learn about agriculture on virtual farm tours. You can often find good videos on YouTube or information on the Oregon State University website.

The White House and Mount Vernon: You can tour homes of presidents virtually. You can go on tours that have 360 degree views. The White House today and Mount Vernon set back in time when George Washington lived there.

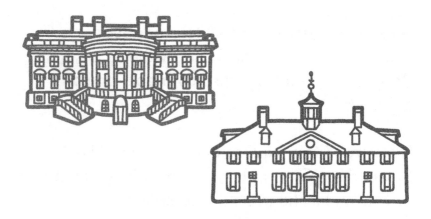

VIRTUAL FIELD TRIP IDEAS

Zoos and Wildlife: Take a virtual trip to zoos and wildlife reserves to observe animals in their natural habitats or in captivity. Live Cams at Zoos capture all different animals, which will encourage kids to write. They can watch their animal in REAL time as they write about it.

Wild Animal Live Cams: Search for live cams in the wild where you can see things like the Djuma Feeding Hole, the African Safari with lots of animals, or live elephant families in Kenya. Other fascinating sites to visit are bears fishing in Alaska. It is quite amazing to watch salmon jumping up stream and bears waiting for their catch. Keep the time difference in mind when watching live feeds from other countries. We would watch elephants at dusk first thing in the morning.

END OF YEAR ACTIVITIES

Paper Airplane Challenge: Each child makes a paper airplane. Then, they throw their airplanes into the air to see who can fly the farthest.

JibJab Videos: It is fun to put students' faces into fun summertime videos. They sing, dance and laugh uncontrollably when they see themselves in a video.

DIY Photo Albums: In the past, I have copied end of year memory books that kids have to fill out including their favorites from the year, but they never seem to get finished because they are burned out. A DIY photo album made from stationary paper, printed pictures, glue sticks, scissors and stickers is a huge hit and a favorite memory of the year. Kids love to reminisce when they look at the photos and years later, they tell me that they still have their photo book.

Teacher Report Card: Let the students grade you on your teaching plus different characteristics about you. It is fun to see what they have to say. Kids of all ages love this activity. I got my copy from Teachers Pay Teacher for only a couple dollars.

INTEGRATE GAMES INTO LESSON PLANS

Align Games with Learning Objectives: Choose games that align with specific learning objectives and concepts you want to reinforce. Games should have clear educational value and connect to the content being taught.

Identify Appropriate Game Types: Select games that suit the age group, interests, and abilities of your students. Consider whether the game is best suited for individual, small group, or whole-class play.

Introduce Games as Review or Warm-up Activities: Use games as a fun way to review previously taught material or as a warm-up activity to get students engaged and focused at the beginning of a lesson.

Designate Game Days: Set aside specific days or periods for game-based learning in your lesson plan. This allows students to anticipate and look forward to the game-based activities.

INTEGRATE GAMES INTO LESSON PLANS

Use Games for Assessment: Incorporate games as formative or summative assessments to gauge students' understanding and progress. Games can provide valuable insights into individual and group learning outcomes. Many often offer data downloads that you can use for grading.

Create Contextual Challenges: Integrate games that require problem-solving and critical thinking within the context of the lesson's content. This helps students apply their knowledge to real-world scenarios.

Gamify Learning Progression: Create a gamified learning progression where students earn points, badges, or rewards for achieving learning milestones. This can foster a sense of achievement and motivation.

Encourage Reflection: After playing games, have students reflect on their experiences, what they learned, and how the game connected to the lesson's objectives.

INTEGRATE GAMES INTO LESSON PLANS

Integrate Digital and Board Games: Utilize a mix of digital and traditional board games to provide diverse and interactive learning experiences.

Encourage Student-Created Games: Let students design their own educational games related to the subject matter. This promotes creativity, critical thinking, and deeper engagement with the material.

Modify Existing Games: Adapt existing games to suit your curriculum. You can modify rules, questions, or materials to align the game with your specific learning goals.

Use Games as Extension Activities: Offer games as optional extension activities for students who finish their assignments early or as extra practice for those who need additional support.

Facilitate Debrief Sessions: Following game play, lead discussions about students' experiences, strategies, and the connections they made between the game and the lesson content.

ASSESSMENT AND EVALUATION OF ENGAGEMENT

Observation: Teachers can observe students during class activities and note their level of participation, attention, and active involvement in discussions and tasks. Although it is hard to see everything, you can get a good feel just by taking a walk around and observing.

Peer Assessment: Students can assess their peers' engagement by providing feedback on their contributions to group work, discussions, or presentations.

Student Self-Assessment: Encourage students to reflect on their own engagement and participation. This can be done through self-assessment surveys or journals where students rate their level of engagement and provide feedback on the class activities.

ASSESSMENT AND EVALUATION OF ENGAGEMENT

Classroom Response Systems: Use classroom response systems like online polling tools to gather real-time feedback on student understanding and engagement during class. Google Classroom has a good question answer poll that is easy to use and fast to get results. If teaching online, Zoom has a good poll system as well.

Exit Tickets: At the end of the class, ask students to respond to a brief question or prompt about the lesson, which provides insight into their level of engagement and understanding. It also gives feedback to see if any reteach or review is necessary.

Engagement Checklists: Develop checklists that outlines specific engagement behaviors such as asking questions, actively listening, and participating in group work. Use the checklist to assess students' engagement during class.

ASSESSMENT AND EVALUATION OF ENGAGEMENT

Informal Check-ins: Have one-on-one or small group conversations with students to discuss their feelings about class engagement and gather insights into potential barriers.

Long-term Progress: Compare students' engagement levels over time to identify trends or changes in their participation.

Frequency of Participation: Track the frequency of each student's participation in class discussions, group activities, and other interactive elements.

Work Samples: Examine students' work samples, projects, and assignments to determine the depth of their engagement and the quality of their contributions.

Attendance and Punctuality: Monitor student attendance and punctuality, as consistent absenteeism or tardiness may indicate disengagement.

COLLECTING STUDENT FEEDBACK

Collecting student feedback is essential for understanding their perspectives, needs, and experiences in the classroom. Here are some effective methods for collecting student feedback.

Anonymous Surveys: Create online or paper-based surveys that allow students to provide feedback anonymously. This encourages honest responses without the fear of judgment.

Classroom Discussions: Engage in open and honest discussions with students about their learning experiences, challenges, and suggestions for improvement.

One-on-One Conferences: Schedule individual conferences with students to discuss their learning progress and gather personalized feedback.

Group Interviews: Conduct focus group interviews with small groups of students to dive deeper into specific topics or concerns.

COLLECTING STUDENT FEEDBACK

Feedback Boxes: Place a feedback box in the classroom where students can drop anonymous written feedback. Have a physical or a virtual suggestion box where students can submit ideas or concerns.

Digital Polls: Use online polling tools to gather real-time feedback on specific topics or questions during class.

Peer Feedback: Encourage students to provide constructive feedback to their peers during group work or presentations.

Reflective Journals: Assign reflective journal writing where students can express their thoughts, feelings, and suggestions regularly, but privately.

Learning Reflections: Incorporate reflection activities in lesson plans, where students assess their learning experiences and identify areas for growth.

COLLECTING STUDENT FEEDBACK

Student-Led Conferences: Allow students to take the lead in parent-teacher conferences, where they can discuss their progress and goals. This helps them to grow and share their learning with families.

Learning Portfolios: Create learning portfolios where students can collect evidence of their progress and self-assess their work.

When collecting student feedback, it's essential to listen actively, respect their opinions, and take their suggestions seriously. Act on the feedback when appropriate and communicate with students about any changes implemented based on their input. By involving students in the feedback process, you create a more student-centered learning environment and demonstrate that their voices are valued.

COLLABORATING WITH COLLEAGUES

By fostering a culture of collaboration and open communication, you can create a strong support network among colleagues, leading to a more engaging and effective learning environment for all students.

Form a Professional Learning Community (PLC): Establish a PLC within your school or department dedicated to discussing engagement strategies, sharing experiences, and supporting one another in implementing them.

Organize Regular Meetings: Schedule regular meetings with your colleagues to discuss engagement techniques and their impact on student learning. Use these meetings as opportunities to brainstorm new ideas and troubleshoot challenges.

Co-Plan Lessons and Activities: Collaborate with a colleague to co-plan and co-teach lessons that incorporate engaging activities. This allows you to observe each other's methods and provide feedback.

COLLABORATING WITH COLLEAGUES

Share Success Stories: Encourage colleagues to share their success stories related to student engagement. Celebrate and learn from each other's achievements.

Create a Shared Resource Bank: Establish a digital platform or shared folder where colleagues can contribute and access engagement resources, such as lesson plans, activities, and games.

Observe Classes: Organize classroom observations to see how different teachers foster engagement in their classrooms. This provides valuable insights and new perspectives. Working with other teachers has always given me take aways. I joined a lesson design workshop team with my teaching partner along with three teachers from another school and it was valuable. Fellow teachers can be our best teachers.

Participate in Professional Development Workshops: Attend workshops and conferences focused on engagement strategies and bring back insights to share with your colleagues.

COLLABORATING WITH COLLEAGUES

Collaborate on Cross-Curricular Projects: Work with colleagues from different subjects to design cross-curricular projects that promote engagement and connections between subjects.

Share Research and Articles: Share relevant research papers, articles, and books on student engagement to keep colleagues informed about the latest trends and findings.

Use Technology for Collaboration: Utilize communication tools and online platforms to facilitate ongoing collaboration and information sharing. Also, be willing to give support to staff members that may need extra help to learn technology.

Offer Support and Encouragement: Be supportive of colleagues' efforts to enhance engagement and encourage them to take risks in trying new approaches

COLLABORATING WITH COLLEAGUES

Celebrate Engaged Learning: Acknowledge and celebrate examples of engaged learning in the classroom, highlighting the positive impact on students.

This shows in the behaviors and attitudes of the kids. Are they happy and thriving? If so, this should reflect in their test scores. Make sure you are looking at student growth, not current level of achievement.

AI IN EDUCATION

Lesson Planning and New Ideas: If you have an idea for a lesson, but don't have the time to research and/or write it, let AI help. Use Chat GPT to find new ideas for the classroom. If you have questions or need lesson ideas, ask Chat GPT. If you don't get what you are looking for, rephrase your question and ask again. To use Chat GPT, just Google it and use your email to sign in. It is worth checking out.

AI for students would come at a later point in time after much teaching and guiding.

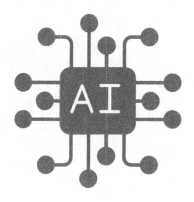

JUST TRY SOMETHING

Just try different classroom engagement games, activities or strategies listed in this book. You will be sure to find ideas that you like and want to use over and over again. It may be something as simple as quiet ball or something much more collaborative. It's up to you, but just try something new to bring your classroom and students to life!

If you have found this book helpful, please leave a review on Amazon. I would greatly appreciate it! If you have any other feedback, please email me!

RESOURCES

If you would like more information about anything mentioned in this book, feel free to email me at heyjodismith@gmail.com and I will be happy to share what I have or more of what I know.

BONUS

Download a free copy of **Levels of Engagement** posters below.

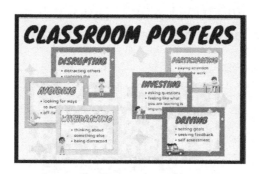

ABOUT THE AUTHOR

My name is Jodi Smith and I live in Oregon with my husband, Ray. We have raised 4 wonderful kids. Teaching is my second career of over 10 years. I am so grateful that I can continue to be with kids every day. I love inspiring kids to love writing, but have really focused on increasing engagement in my own classroom over the past several years. I have taken advantage of professional development opportunities and research. I also use social media including TikTok and Pinterest. This effort has transformed my classroom from boring to buzzing!

Made in the USA
Las Vegas, NV
22 August 2024

94309896R00057